S.C & H.C IMPORTANT CASE LAWS

S.C & H.C IMPORTANT CASE LAWS

NITIN MASKE

Contents

CHAPTER I

SC and H.C important judgments

1. **A.R. Antulay vs R.S. Nayak & Anr Supreme Court ,1988 AIR 1531, 1988 SCR Supl. (1)** : If a mistake is detected then Courts (even SC) can correct it later.
2. **A. Jayachandra vs Aneel Kaur Supreme Court (2005) 2 SCC 22 :** Acts subsequent to the filing of the petition can be taken note of to show a pattern in the behaviour and conduct.
3. **A.V. Papayya Sastry & Ors vs Government Of A.P. & Ors Supreme Court 07 March 2007 (2007) 4 SCC 211 :** 1. Order taken by fraud or suppressing material fact can be recalled at any stage of litigation (using CPC 151 or CrPC 482) , 2. Once a Superior court accepts an appeal, lower courts cannot recall or proceed with the Litigation.
4. **Abbayolla M. Subba Reddy vs Padmamma Andhra HC ,1998 (5) ALD 465, 1998 (5) ALT 152, I (2000) DMC 266 :** 1.If marriage is nullity, then HMA 25 not applicable. 2.Court cannot grant relief of maintenance obtainable under one Act in proceedings under the other.
5. **Abdul Rub & Ors. vs Razia Begum Delhi HC, 2010 :** Every relative of the husband cannot be made as a respondent.
6. **Abhijit Pawar vs Hemant Madhukar Nimbalkar Supreme Court (2017) 3 SCC 528** : an obligation is cast on the learned Magistrate to ensure before summoning the accused who resides beyond his jurisdiction, to make necessary enquiry.
7. **Advocate Ramesh vs State of Maharshtra Bombay HC 13 June 2011** : For DV temporary residing doesnt mean casual stay.
8. **Afcons Infrastructure Ltd. vs Cherian Varkey Construction Co Supreme Court (2010) 8 SCC 24** : Explains Alternative Dispute Resolution (Arbitration, judicial settlement,Lok Adalat, Mediation).
9. **Alika Khosla vs Thomas Mathew And Anr 1996 Delhi HC II (1996) DMC 218** : Audio recording with Transcript admissible as evidence.
10. **Alika Khosla vs Thomas Mathew And Anr 2001 Delhi HC 2002 (62) DRJ 851 :** Right to Privacy is not Absolute.
11. **Alok Kumar Jain Vs. Purnima Jain Delhi HC AIR 2007 (NOC) 1654 (Del.), 2007(96) DRJ 115** : Things to rely on while awarding interim

maintenance.

12. **Amarawati And Anr. vs State Of U.P Allahabad HC 2005 (1) AWC 416, 2005 CriLJ 755, (2005) 1 UPLBEC 155** : 1.Hierarchy of laws 2. Arrest is not a must whenever an F.I.R. of a cognizable offence is lodged. 3. any application for bail under Section 437, CrPC should ordinarily be decided by the Magistrate the same day, except in rare cases where reasons shall be recorded in writing for adjourning the hearing of the bail application.
13. **Amit Agarwal And Ors vs Sanjay Aggarwal And Ors Punjab-Haryana HC 31 May 2016** : DV cant be filed after Divorce.
14. **Amit Khanna vs Priyanka Khanna & Ors Delhi HC 2010 (119) DRJ 182** : Claim of high status of husband not sufficient for interim maintenance.
15. **Anil Jain vs Maya Jain Supreme Court (2009)10 SCC 415** : Wife retracts after filing MCD and taking valuables under MCD terms, husband approaches SC. SC allows divorce on MCD.
16. **Anshu Gupta vs State (Nct Of Delhi) Delhi District Court** : Judgment is passed only on affidavits. Parties have not been given the opportunity to cross-examine each others witnesses. So went back for trial.
17. **Anu Kaul vs Rajeev Kaul Supreme Court (2009) 13 SCC 209** : Wife working no maintenance.
18. **Anuradha Alias Chanchal Kumari vs Santoshnath Khanna Delhi HC ILR 1977 Delhi 739, 1978 RLR 111** : A particular kind of impotency known as Impotentia quoad hunc vel ham. That is to say incapacity to perform coitus with a particular individual. A party is impotent if his or her mental or physical condition makes consummation of the marriage a practical impossibility.
19. **Anurag Anand vs Sunita Anand Delhi HC 1997 IAD Delhi 37, AIR 1997 Delhi 94, 65 (1997) DLT 1037, II (1996) DMC 389, 1997 (40) DRJ 68** : Judgement Against Husband = Husband gives wrong Salary and family property details in biodata, hence Wife took Annulment.
20. **Archana Gupta vs Rajeev Gupta Uttarakhand HC** : No Maintenance u/s Crpc 125 if wife deserts husband.
21. **Arnesh Kumar vs State Of Bihar & Anr Supreme Court (2014) 8 SCC 273** : Police should justify their arrest and should not arrest without reason.
22. **Arun Atmaram Patil & Ors vs Sandhya Arun Patil & Anr Bombay HC 24 February 2016** : When one party has acted on the consent terms to it's disadvantage, the other party having received the benefits cannot be

allowed to backtrack

23. **Arun Kashinath Deshpande Vs. Inumati Ramchandra Deo Bombay HC 08 April 2010 LAWS(BOM)- 2010-4-252** : Wife was earning and she suppressed this so permanent alimony cancelled.
24. **Arun Kumar Agarwal vs Radha Arun Karnataka HC PERJURY 15 March 2001 CriLJ 3561** : Petition under CrPC 340 must be decided only at the end.
25. **Arvind Kumar Prasad vs Geeta Prasad Patna HC HMA 13 1(ia) 15 March 2017** : Wife filed 498A and made various scandalous allegations, Divorce on cruelty.
26. **Asha Devi vs Pominder Kumar Chhabra Delhi HC HMA 24 07 September 2006** : Judgement Against Husband = Maint to be paid till the till HMA petition not terminated.
27. **Ashok Yeshwant Samant vs Smt. Suparna Ashok Samant Bombay HC 1991 (1) BomCR 383, (1990) 92 BOMLR 434, 1991 CriLJ 766, II (1991) DMC 132** : Recovery under 125(3) are independent of 127, thus Husband cannot be directed to deposit the arrear as condition to proceed wih his applicationof 127.
28. **B.P. Achala Anand Vs S.Appi Reddy & Anr Supreme Court (2005) 3 SCC 313** : Right to Residence after Divorce to be decided based on Divorce Terms.
29. **B.Prakash vs Deepa Madras HC 28 July 2015** : DV and 125 cant be filed on the same set of allegations and cause of action.
30. **Bai Bhanbai Mavji vs Kanbi Karshan Devraj And Anr Gujarat HC HMA 11 AIR 1970 Guj 137, 1970 CriLJ 962, (1970) 0 GLR 581** : Wife not eligible for Maint if it falls under HMA 11.
31. **Bhadrayu C Vachharajani VS Saurashtra University Gujarat HC 29 November 2013 GHJ-2014-35-385** : If court has no Jurisdiciton, it cannot go into Meritts of case.
32. **Bhagwan Dutt vs Kamla Devi Supreme Court 1975 AIR 83,1975 SCR (2) 483** : Separate income of the wife can be taken into account in determining the amount of maintenance payable to her.
33. **Bhagwan Raoji Dale vs Sushma Alias Nanda Bhagwan Dale Bombay HC 1999 (5) BomCR 851, I (1999) DMC 168** : Deserting wife NOT entitled to maint us 125 CrPC. NOT entitled after divorce also.
34. **Bhaurao Shankar Lokhande & Anr vs State Of Maharashtra & Anr Supreme Court 1965 AIR 1564, 1965 SCR (2) 837** : If the marriage is not a valid marriage, it is no marriage in the eye of law.

35. **Bhausaheb Magar vs Leelabai Magar 2003 Bombay HC AIR 2004 Bom 283, II (2004) DMC 321, 2003 (4) MhLj 1019** : No Permanent Alimony in Sec 11, Permanent Alimony may be asked in sec 12.
36. **Bhausaheb Magar vs Leelabai Magar 2006 Bombay HC AIRBOMR200727 11, ALLMR20073676 , LAWS(BOM)200 611179** : Doctrine of res judicata.
37. **Bheekha Ram vs Goma Devi And Ors Rajasthan HC I (2000) DMC 76, 1999 WLC Raj UC 260** : No maintenance for a deserting wife
38. **Bhushan Kumar Meen vs Mansi Meen @ Harpreet Kaur Supreme Court (2010) 15 SCC 372** : House Loan EMI to be considered while granting interim maint.
39. **Capt Dr Hamesh Kumar Vs Dr Nisha Sahi Punjab-Haryana HC CURLJ-1993-2- 367, LAWS(P&H)-1993-7-125** : Wife Working, taking unnecessary adjournments, Quashed under CrPC 482
40. **Chand Dhawan vs Jawaharlal Dhawan Supreme Court 1993 SCR (3) 954, 1993 SCC (3) 406** : Court cannot grant relief of maintenance obtainable under one Act in proceedings under the other.
41. **Chander Bhan vs State of Delhi Delhi HC 04 August 2008 :** Guideline for 498A cases.
42. **Chandra Shashi vs Anil Kumar Verma Supreme Court 1995 SCC (1) 421, JT 1994 (7) 459** : No one should indulge in immoral acts like perjury, prevarication and motivated falsehoods : 2 weeks Jail.
43. **Chandrakala Alias Vandana vs Subhash Dhondiba Gaokhandkar Bombay HC (1994) 96 BOMLR 726** : Wife was suffering from leprosy since prior to marriage.This material fact concealed hence Annulment. Wife may seek Alimony.
44. **Chaturbhuj vs Sita Bai Supreme Court 27 November 2007 (2008) 2 SCC 316** : Where the personal income of the wife is insufficient she can claim maintenance under Section 125 Cr.P.C.
45. **Chhandupriya @ Priyanka vs Rahul Mahod Bombay HC - Nagpur 17 March 2016** : Wife has a lover from prior to marriage and marriage was not consummated.
46. **Chiranjeev Kumar Arya vs State Of U.P. & Another Allahabad HC** : 1. Revisional power of High Court under 482 CrPC held intact under the DV act. 2. fraud avoids all judicial acts, ecclesiastical or temporal.
47. **Commissioner Of Income-Tax vs Godavaridevi Saraf Bombay HC 1978 (2) ELT 624 Bom, 1978 113 ITR 589 Bom :** Tribunal (or court) anywhere in the country has to respect the law laid down by the High

Court, though of a different State, so long as there is no contrary decision of any other High Court on that question.

48. **D.Velusamy vs D.Patchaiammal Supreme Court AIR(SC)-2011-0- 479, SCC-2010-10-469,ALLSCR 2010-0-2639** : Relationship in the nature of marriage for DV Act.
49. **Dalip Singh vs State Of U.P. & Ors Supreme Court 03 December 2009 (2010) 2 SCC 114** : No Relief if Litigant lies OR supress material fact and came with Unclean Hands.
50. **Damanpreet Kaur vs Indermeet Juneja & Anr Delhi HC (2013) 1 JCC 306** : Well educated earning wife, resigned on her own will, maint declined.
51. **Deb Narayan Halder vs Anushree Halder Supreme Court (2003) 11 SCC 303** : wife who leaves matrimonial home without any justification is not entitled to maintenance under Section 125.
52. **Deepak @ Gajanan Ramrao Kanegaonkar vs Soniya Depak Bombay HC 01 July 2015 :** Women lived in with a married person even after knowing that he is married, hence this relation cannot be the one as in marriage, so DV denied to women and child.
53. **Deoki Panjhiyara v. Shashi Bhushan Narayan Azad Supreme Court AIR(SC)- 2013-0- 346, (2013) 2 SCC 137** : Judgement against Husband = Until Marriage is declared Null, Wife is wife.
54. **Dimple Khanna vs Anita Advani Bombay HC 09 April 2015** : 1. For DV Relationship in the nature of marriage is a must.2. Relatives who did not shared household cant be made respondents.
55. **E. Shanthi vs Dr. H.K. Vasudev Karnataka HC AIR 2005 Kant 417, ILR 2005 KAR 4981** : Wife was qualified and working before marriage. She is capable of earning, hence maint declined.
56. **Foreshore Co-Op.Hng.Society Ltd vs Praveen D Desai Supreme Court 08 April 2015** : Discussion on Jurisdiction.
57. **G. Padmini vs G. Sivananda Babu Andhra H 2000 (2) ALD 258, 2000 (2) ALT 259, II (2000) DMC 760** : Divorce on Cruelty as wife's letter to others regarding husband's impotency was cruelty.
58. **G. Ramanathan vs Revathy Madras HC 1989 Crl.LJ 2037 (1)** : Wife cannot seek the same relief from JM court when matter is pending in Civil Court.
59. **G. Shyamala Ranjini vs M.S. Tamizhnathan Madras HC** : Related to Audio CD as Evidence..

60. **G.V.N. Kameswara Rao vs G. Jabilli Supreme Court 2002 AIR SCW 162, (2002) 2 SCC 296** : Husband files Divorce on Mental Cruelty as Wife left husband and refused to return. Wife also filed police complaint. Wife pleaded to dismiss divorce using HMA 23(1)(a) but Divorce granted but with Alimony.
61. **Geeta Singh Deo vs State Of Rajasthan Rajasthan HC - Jaipur 17 November 2016 :** Well Educated (PG) Woman (Daughter) cant seek maint (for further high studies) unless DV has occurred.
62. **Gian Chand vs Dilpreet Kaur Punjab-Haryana HC 23 February 2010** : Maintenance awarded in two sections to be offset.
63. **Gurbinder Singh vs Manjit Kaur Delhi HC 25 January 2010** : Wife after concealing the material facts about her own employment and agreement with husband, took exparte order in her favour, so contempt and fine.
64. **Gurudev Gurav vs Jayashree Karnataka HC 08 January 2014** : Limitation of DV is one year from cause of action.
65. **Harminder Kaur vs Gurtar Singh Punjab-Haryana HC 17 February 2011** : Maintenance pendente lite and expenses of proceedings not for those who have income sufficient for support and the necessary expenses.
66. **Haunsabai vs Balkrishna Krishna Badigar Karnataka HC 1981 CriLJ 110, ILR 1980 KAR 612, 1980 (2) KarLJ 158** : Wife should prove that she is unable to maintain herself in addition to the facts that her husband has sufficient means to maintain her and that he has neglected to maintain her.
67. **Harpreet Kaur VS Dilvinder Singh Bedi Mahila Court Delhi 24 May 2011** : Husband lost job because of complaint, maintenance denied.
68. **Havovi Kersi Sethna vs Kersi Gustad Sethna Bombay HC 28 January 2011** :Details on how CD can be made admissible in court.
69. **Hemlataben vs State Gujrat HC DV 21 October 2010** : Interim maintenance in DV is refused as Wife was working.
70. **Hima Chugh vs Pritam Ashok Sadaphule Delhi HC (2013) DMC 649 (Del.)** : Protection order could be obtained only against a person who was in domestic relationship with the person aggrieved.
71. **Hiral P. Harsora And Ors vs Kusum Narottamdas Harsora And Ors Supreme Court (2016) 10 SCC 165** : DV can be filed by any woman on any relative who subjected her to DV.
72. **Hussain and Anr vs Union of India with Aasu vs State of Rajasthan Supreme Court 09 March 2017** : 1. Speedy trial is a part of reasonable,

fair and just procedure guaranteed under Article 21. 2. Bail application to be disposed in a week.

73. **Inderjit Singh Grewal vs State Of Punjab & Anr Supreme Court AIR(SCW)-2011-0-6259, SCC-2011- 12-588** : 1 Year limit to DV.
74. **Indra Sarma vs V.K.V.Sarma Supreme Court (2013(4) K.L.T. 763), Manu/SC/1230/20 13, AIR 2014 SC 309, 2013 (9) LRC 1 (SC)** : All live-in- relationships are not relationships in the nature of marriage.
75. **Ines Miranda Vs Santosh K Swamy Supreme Court 14 December 2009** : Wife (working) filed Divorce, Husband (unemployed) filed RCR. Court transfers case at Wife's city on the condition that she will pay Maint. For jobless Husband.
76. **Jaiprakash Madhukarrao Sahurkar vs Sarika Bombay HC 29 February 2016** : Judgement Against Husband = DV and 498A can be filed on same facts.
77. **Iqbal Bano vs State Of U.P. And Anr Supreme Court AIR 2007 SC 2215** : 1. Section 125 Cr.P.C.Proceedings under are civil in nature. 2. Divorce Muslim Wife is eligible for Maint under 125.
78. **Jagdish Prasad vs State & Others Delhi HC 23 March 2009** : Wife lied related to her working status hence Perjury allowed.
79. **Jamboo Parasad Jain vs Smt. Malti Prabha And Anr. Allahabad HC 24 January 1979 AIR 1979 All 260**: HMA 15 not apllicable in HMA 11 OR 12 80
80. **Jangam Srinivasa Rao vs Jangam Rajeswarin Andhra HC 1990 CriLJ 2506** : Maximum period for which Wife can claim maintenance under the procedure contemplated under S. 125(3) is one year.
81. **Jayanti Deb Das vs Manas Kumar Das Tripura HC AIR 2015 Tripura 25** : The allegation of adultery made by the wife appellant and not proved is nothing but mental cruelty.
82. **Jayesh Uttamrao Khairnar vs State of Maharashtra.pdf Bombay HC - Aurangabad 2010 ALL MR (Cri) 2259** : Husband got divorce after a separation of one year. After divorce wife filed DV hence not maintainable as Domestic Relation is absent.
83. **Joginder Kumar vs State Of U.P Supreme Court 1994 AIR 1349, 1994 SCC (4) 260** : No arrest can be made because it is lawful for the police officer to do so. The existence of the power to arrest is one thing. The justification for the exercise of it is quite another.No arrest can be made in a routine manner on a mere allegation of commission of an offence made against a person.

84. **Joginder vs State Nct Of Delhi & Anr Delhi HC 2010 (119) DRJ 349** : Interim Maintenance formula evolved by judge (2:1::husband:dependent).
85. **Justyn Cyril vs Hannah Vasanthie Madras HC II (1994) DMC 545, (1994) IMLJ 17** : From the time of the marriage, the Wife was not willing to have intercourse with the husband, hence Annulled.
86. **Jyoti Singh vs Yogendra Singh Supreme Court** : Divorce by husband was transferred to Wife's city but all cases were to be taken together.
87. **K. Srinivas vs K. Sunita Supreme Court 19 November 2014 (2014) 16 SCC 34** : Wife had filed a false criminal complaint, and even one such complaint is sufficient to constitute matrimonial cruelty. Hence Divorce.
88. **K.Srinivas Rao vs D.A. Deepa Supreme Court (2013) 5 SCC 226** : Divorce on Cruelty as Wife had filed a criminal complaint and sent letters to employer of husband. But with Huge Alimony.
89. **K.Subhadra Patra Vs Mosomat K Aadiya Amma & Ors Supreme Court** : One can file counter affidavit by post.
90. **K.V. Prakash Babu vs State Of Karnataka Supreme Court 22 November 2016** : Adultery is not Cruelty for 498A.
91. **Kamini Sondhi vs Kapil Sondhi Delhi HC 09 September 2016** : Sexless marriage, Wife made false complaints to husband's boss, hence Divorce on mental cruelty.
92. **Kavita Prasad vs Ram Ashray Prasad Delhi HC 01 October 2008** : Qualified wife sitting idle and claiming maint. From husband should go and do work for society free of charge as long as she is claiming maint on acccount of being unemployed.
93. **Kavita vs Harish Raisen Madhya Pradesh HC 2006 (2) MPHT 515** : Divorce on Cruelty as Wife had filed a criminal complaint.
94. **Kiran Bala Asthana And Anr. vs Bhaire Prasad Srivastava Allahabad HC AIR 1982 All 242** : Wife was suffering from Mental Illness.This material fact concealed hence Annulment. Wife may seek Alimony.
95. **Kiran Dutta vs State & Anr Delhi HC 11 February 2014** : DIR is a must before passing orders under Sec 12 of DV.
96. **Kolla Veera Raghav Rao vs Gorantla Venkateswara Rao And Anr Supreme Court 01 February 2011** : Section 300(1) of Cr.P.C. states that no one can be tried and convicted for the same offence or even for a different offence but on the same facts.
97. **Koushik Vs Sangeeta Koushik Gharami Bombay HC - Nagpur 05 May 2014** : No Maint in DV to wife or Children if DV not proved.

98. **Krishnamurthy Nookula vs Savitha Y Karnataka HC 09 December 2009** : Enquiry is required where case is not ex-parte.
99. **Kusum Sharma vs Mahinder Kumar Sharma Delhi HC 2014 (214) DLT 493** : Not Good for Husbands if wife is not working = Detailed Affidavit required for income and expenditure in matrimonial cases.
100. **Kumaresan vs Aswathi Madras HC 21 June 2002 (2002) 2 MLJ 760** : Sufficiently Earning wife not eligible for HMA 24.
101. **Kunaldev Singh Rathore vs State Of M.P Madhya Pradesh HC 02 December 2016** : Defence Documents May Be Examined At Preliminary Stage, If Needed. Under Section 482 CrPC the court is free to consider material that may be produced on behalf of the accused to arrive at a decision whether the charge as framed could be maintained.
102. **Lal Kamlendra Pratap Singh vs State Of U.P Supreme Court 23 March 2009 (2009) 4 SCC 437** : 1. the Court, if it deems fit in the facts and circumstances of the case, may grant interim bail pending final disposal of the bail application. 2. arrest is not a must whenever an F.I.R. of a cognizable offence is lodged.
103. **Lalita Kumari vs Govt.Of U.P.& Ors Supreme Court 2014 (2) SCC 1** : Preliminary inquiry may be made before Registering FIR in Matrimonial Matters.If, after investigation, the information given is found to be false, there is always an option to prosecute the complainant for filing a false FIR.
104. **Laljee Yadav vs The State Of Bihar Patna HC 16 September 2001 2011 (4) PLJR 248** : 1. Before the wife can claim maintenance she must show that she is unable to maintain herself and that her husband has sufficient means but neglects or refuses to maintain. 2. Distress warrant for recovery cant be initiated straightaway before issuing a warrant for levying the amount due in the manner provided for levying fines. 3. there has to be separate sentencing upon separate and fresh application after considering the matter for each month or part thereof for which maintenance remains unpaid. Thus, by no stretch of imagination, can there be a continuous mechanical remand.
105. **M vs M Bombay HC 07 February 2014 :** Divorce on Cruelty as Wife had filed a criminal complaint. Wife could not prove her allegations in WS, Option open for applying maint in sec 25 of HMA.
106. **M. Srinivasulu Vs State Of A.P. Supreme Court 10 September 2007 AIR 2007 SC 3146 :** SC Defines 498A , 304B & Dowry.

107. **Maganti Kanakadurga vs Maganti Venkateswarlu Andhra HCAIR 2006 AP 259, 2006 (4) ALD 411** : consummation has not taken place and as already referred it was on account of the appellant's repugnancy for consummation and probably on account of her reluctance towards consummation due to her physical disability of not having attained puberty.
108. **Maharashtra Government VS Rajaram Digamber Padamwar Bombay HC 08 April 2011 LAWS(BOM)201 1410 ALLMR(CRI)201 101825 BCR(CRI)201136 40 , FAC20112278 :** HC takes actiona against a trial court judge who went against a previous HC precedent and declined to abide by it.
109. **Mahila Vinod Kumari vs State Of M.P Supreme Court (2008) 8 SCC 34** : Petitioner had tendered false evidence and had fabricated evidence against the accused persons with the intention that such evidence shall be used in the proceedings.
110. **Malathi Ravi vs B.V. RaviSupreme CourtHMA 13 1(ia)30 June 20142014 7 SCC 64** :Divorce on Cruelty as Wife had filed a criminal complaint. But with Huge Maint for Child.
111. **Mamta Jaiswal vs Rajesh JaiswalMadhya Pradesh HC II (2000) DMC 170** : Well qualified woman with past work experience cant sit idle and claim maint.
112. **Mangesh Balkrushna Bhoir vs Sau. Leena Mangesh BhoirBombay HC 23 December 2015** : Divorce on Cruelty as Wife had filed a criminal complaint.
113. **Manish Kapoor vs Charu KapoorDelhi District Court** : It explains Procedure to be followed in DV and 125.
114. **Manish Kumar vs Pratibha Delhi HC 18 September 2008** : No Maintenance u/s HMA 24 for working Women.
115. **Manisha Tyagi vs Deepak KumarSupreme Cour I (2010) DMC 451 (SC)** : Cruelty not proved, but both party were at fault hence judicial separation.
116. **Manju Kamal Mehra vs Kamal Pushkar MehraBombay HC 18 July 2009** : Wife not entitiled to maint as HMA 9 was in husband's favour.
117. **Manoj Kumar Saini vs CPIOCICCPC24 March 2011** : ITR can be given in criminal case against the State pertaining to dowry related issues because public interest in the administration of justice in a particular case overrides all other aspects of public interest,

118. **Manoj Kumar Soni vs Deepti SoniMadhya Pradesh HC 17 September 2014** : Divorce on Cruelty as wife makes many false allegations and also termed husband as impotent, ill treatement to husband's parents.
119. **Manoj Yadav vs Pushpa @ Kiran Yadav & Ors.Supreme Court 11 January 2011** : Different Maxm Quantum of maintenance fixed by different States by way of State amendments held to be unconstitutional.
120. **Manokaran @ Ramamoorthy vs M. DevakiMadras HC 21 February 2003AIR 2003 Mad 212, I (2003)DMC 799, (2003) 1 MLJ 752** : Sufficiently Earning wife not eligible for HMA 24
121. **Marimuthu vs Janaki Madras HC 22 February 2008** : Couple was living separately by mutual consent, hence maint denied.
122. **Mayadevi vs Jagdish Prasad Supreme Court AIR 2007 SC 1426** : 1. Divorce on Cruelty as wife makes many false allegations and also termed husband as impotent, ill treatement to husband's parents. 2.Standard of proof beyond reasonable doubt not required in matrimonial disputes.
123. **Meena Dinesh Parmar vs Dinesh Hastimal Parmar Bombay HC AIR 2005 Bom 298, 2005 (4) BomCR 672, 2005 (2) MhLj 305** : Maintenence not granted as it is proved that wife wants to reside separately.
124. **Meena Dinesh Parmar vs Dinesh Hastimal ParmarBombay HC AIR 2005 Bom 298, 2005 (4) BomCR 672, 2005 (2) MhLj 305** : Wife was living at her Maternal Uncle's place and refused to return. Maintenance not granted as it is proved that wife wants to reside separately.
125. **Moina Khosla vs Amardeep Singh Khosla Delhi HC AIR 1986 Delhi 399, 1986 (10) DRJ 286** : As no sexual intercourse has taken place between the parties, in this case, the requirements of Section 12(1)(a) of the Act are satisfied.
126. **Monica Bedi vs State Of A.P Supreme Court (2011) 1 SCC 284** : Double jeopardy applies to punishment for same offence, not same facts.
127. **Monika Sharma vs Kuldeep Kumar Dogra Himachal Pradesh HC 31 July 2015** : Serious And Unsubstantiated Allegations Of Adultery Amount To Cruelty Offering A Ground For Divorce.
128. **N G Dastane vs S Dastane Supreme Court AIR 1975 SC 1534, (1975) 2 SCC 326, 1975 3 SCR 967** : Judgement Against Husband = Wife was guilty of Cruelty but husband condoned it, subsequent conduct of wife is not a revival of the original cause of action, so Separation denied.
129. **Nachhattar Singh Alias Khanda vs State Of Punjab Punjab-Haryana HC 2009(4) R.C.R. (Criminal) 409** : False case was filed and Men Prosecuted. Later on found innocent so compensated by State for

Damages.

130. **Narendra vs K.Meena Supreme Court 06 October 2016** : unsubstantiated allegations of relations levelled by wife and the threats and attempt to commit suicide by her amounted to mental cruelty.

131. **Narinder Pal Kaur Vs. Manjeet Singh Delhi HC AIR 2008 Delhi 7, 148 (2008) DLT 522, I (2008) DMC 529** : Second wife entitiled for Maint. Under HAMA section 18.

132. **Natasha Singh vs CBI (State) Supreme Court (2013) 5 SCC 741** : Section 311 Cr.P.C. empowers the court to summon a material witness, or to examine a person present at "any stage" of "any enquiry", or "trial", or "any other proceedings" under the Cr.P.C., or to summon any person as a witness, or to recall and re-examine any person

133. **Naveen Kohli vs Neelu Kohli Supreme Court 2006 (4) SCC 558.** : Irretrievable breakdown of the marriage.Wife filed multiple cases on husband, SC grants divorce to husband on mental cruelty ground. But high Maint.

134. **Neelam Abhijeet Kadam vs State of Maharashtra Bombay HC 02 May 2017** : Court has to accept pleadings in english and cant force it to be in vernacular language.

135. **Neetu Mittal Vs. Kanta Mittal Delhi HC 2008 (106) DRJ 6223, 2008 (4) RCR (C) 630** : Parents can kickout their Children. Definition of Shared Household and Matrimonial Home.

136. **Niraj Trivedi vs State Of Bihar And Ors Delhi HC 2008 (3) JCC 154** : FIR to be registered at place of crime.

137. **Nishant Hussain vs Seema Saddique & Anr Rajasthan HC -Jodhpur 2012 Law Suit (Raj) 1101** : One completely isolated incidence is not DV.

138. **Nitin Ramesh Dhiwar vs Roopali Nitin Dhiwar Bombay HC 16 August 2012** : filing of a false criminal complaint itself amounts to cruelty within the meaning of section 13(i)

139. **1P.V. Gopalkrishnan vs Kanaksha Gopalkrishnan Bombay HC 1982 (1) BomCR 454 a** : Wife was suffering from sexual disorder. This material fact concealed hence Annulment. Wife may seek Alimony.

140. **Padmja Sharma vs Ratan Lal Sharma Supreme Court 2000 (2) SCR 621** : If wife is working, liability of Child to be taken care by both parents.

141. **Pankaj Mahajan vs Dimple @ Kajal Supreme Court (2011) 12 SCC 1** : giving repeated threats to commit suicide amounts to cruelty.

142. **P.Kalyanasundaram vs K.Paquialatchamy Madras HC AIR 2004 Madras 43, (2003) 1 MLJ 669 (Division Bench)** : Judgement Against

Husband = Alimony can be granted even to an erring spouse.

143. **Pranab Kumar Chakraborty vs Kumkum Chakraborty Calcutta HC (2006) 1 CALLT 210 HC, 2005 (4) CHN 146** : Wife filed false 498A, Husband filed for Divorce on Cruelty but got Divorce on Irretrievable broken marriage. Wife got huge Alimony.

144. **Preeti Gupta & Anr vs State Of Jharkhand & Anr Supreme Court 2010 (3) GLH 258, (2010) 7 SCC 667** : Courts admits misuse of 498A in many cases and quashes the case as Respondent never stayed with complainant. A very Similar case.

145. **Preeti Jain vs Kunal Jain &Anr Rajasthan HC 27 May 2016** : Privilege communication between husband and wife is admissible in family court proceedings.

146. **Pritam Ashok Sadaphule and others VS State of Maharashtra and another Supreme Court 19 March 2015** : Wife files DV at Delhi and 498A at Mumbai on same allegations and facts, SC directs both the case to be tried by one court.

147. **Priyanka Srivastava Vs State of Uttar Pradesh Supreme Court (2015) 6 SCC 287** : Preliminary inquiry may be made in 156(3), 156 (3) applications are to be supported by an affidavit.

148. **Putuli Das vs Dina Nath Talukdar Gauhati HC AIR 2008 Gau 74** : One should give all the facts and grounds in pleading. Giving it later weakens the case.

149. **R.Logeswari vs K.Arul Jothi Madras HC 20 December 2016** : Wife filed Annulment and then asked for transfer to her hometown, Wife was earlier working so Transfer request declined as she was treated as independent.

150. **Rachna Kathuria vs Ramesh Kathuria Delhi HC 2010 (7) R.C.R. (Cr.) 1748, 173 (2010) DLT 289** : Wife already getting maint in 125, hence DV dismissed. Wife has option to enhance maint in 127.

151. **Raj Deo Sharma vs The State Of Bihar Supreme Court AIR 1996 SC 3281, 1998 (5) Scale 477; JT 1998 (7) SC 1** : Right of speedy justice is a fundamental right as envisaged under Article 21 of the Constitution.

152. **Raj Kumar Singh @ Raju @ Batya vs State Of Rajasthan Supreme Court IPC (2013) 5 SCC 722** : if two views are possible on the evidence adduced in the case one pointing to the guilt of the accused and the other to his innocence, the view which is favourable to the accused should be adopted.

153. **Rajan Parmar vs Mamta Parmar District Court Delhi 10 March 2016** : Wife more educated than husband, husband will give maint to wife for one year within which wife has to seek job.
154. **Renuka vs Rajendra Hada Rajasthan HC AIR 2007 Raj 112, RLW 2007 (3) Raj 1839** : 1.appellant expressed her unwillingness to get examined by the medical expert, learned Family Court was entitled to draw the adverse inference against her declaring the marriage of appellant and respondent as null and void 2. marriage could not be consummated owing to the hysteria or extreme sensibility of the wife and there was no question of any structural defect.
155. **Rajasi @ Swapna vs Shashank Dandge Bombay HC - Nagpur 06 January 2015** : Annulment cum Divorce Allowed. Marriage consummated, suicidal traits in the wife so Divorce Allowed.
156. **Rama Kanta Vs Mohinder Laxmidas Bhandula Punjab-Haryana HC AIR 1996 P H 98 :** Consent For Marriage Was Taken By Hiding Imp Facts, Wife was Cruel, so Annulment and Divorce was granted.
157. **Rameshchandra Rampratapji Daga vs Rameshwari Rameshchandra Daga Supreme Court 13 December 2004 AIR 2005 SC 422** : Judgement against Husband = Maint under HMA 25 is applicable in HMA 9 to 13 including 11, 12.
158. **Ramjas Foundation & Ors vs Union Of India & Ors Supreme Court 2010(14) SCC 38 = 2010(15) SCR 364 = 2010(12) JT 134 = 2010(11) SCALE 598** : Unclean Hands, no Relief to be given by any court.
159. **Rampyari & Ors. vs Ms. Kamlesh Delhi HC** : Fine for Delaying tactics by Lawyer
160. Ravindra Haribhau Karmarkar vs Shaila Ravindra Karmarkar Bombay HC 1992 CriLJ 1845 : Wife cannot claim same relief from JM and Civil Court simultaneously.
161. **Rayala M. Bhuvaneswari vs Nagaphanender Rayala Andhra HC AIR 2008 AP 98, 2008 (2) ALD 311, 2008 (1) ALT 613** : Act of tapping itself by the husband of the conversation of his wife with others was illegal and it infringed the right of privacy of the wife.
162. **Renu Mittal vs Anil Mittal & Ors Delhi HC 2010 (7) R.C.R. (Cr.)** : No parallel relief in 125 CrPC & DV for maintenence.
163. **Rita Markandey vs Surjit Singh Arora Supreme Court (1996) 6 SCC 14** : Filing false affidavits is criminal contempt of Court.
164. **Rita Nijhawan vs Balakishan Nijhawan Delhi HC AIR 1973 Delhi 200, 9 (1973) DLT 222** : Detailed meaning of Sex, Consummation,

Intercourse and Cruelty.

165. **Ritu Raj Kant vs Anita Delhi HC 154 (2008) DLT 505** : Maintenance on actual earnings.

166. **Rohtash Singh vs Ramendri And Ors Supreme Court 2000 (2) SCR 58** : Wife is not entitled for maintenance prior to divorce on desertion and cruelty but after Divorce Wife can seek maint.

167. **Rupali Gupta vs Rajat Gupta Delhi HC 05 September 2016** : Qualified working wife not entitled for maint under HMA 24.

168. **S.P Chengalvaraya Naidu vs Jagannath Supreme Court 1994 AIR 853, 1994 SCC (1) 1** : Judgment or decree obtained by playing fraud on the court is a nullity and non exist in the eyes of law.

169. **S.R. Batra vs Taruna Batra Supreme Court I (2007) SLT 1** : Wife has no Right on Husband's parent's Property.

170. **S.Ramesh vs MS.Cethar Ltd Madras HC 12 January 2016** : a person who enjoyed the benefit of an interim order, is liable to compensate the other party, when the main case is decided against him.

171. **Sadhana Satish Kolvankar vs Satish Sachidanand Kolvankar Bombay HC 2005 (2) BomCR 340, 2005 (1) MhLj 935** : Wife refused coitus, broke Mangalsutra, filed 498A, Divorce on Cruelty, high Alimony.

172. **Sadhana Srivastava vs Sri Arvind Kumar Srivastava Allahabad HC AIR 2006 All 7, 2006 (1) AWC 177, II (2005)DMC 863** : Divorce on Cruelty as Wife had filed a criminal complaint. But with Maint.

173. **Samar Ghosh vs. Jaya Ghosh Supreme Court (2007) 4 SCC 511** : Enumerated illustrations of mental cruelty in detail wrt diff country laws.

174. **Samaydin vs State of UP Allahabad HC 04 January 2001 LAWS(ALL)-2001-1-47** : In normal circumstances the maintenance must be granted from the date of the order.

175. **Sangitaben Rasiklal Jaiswal vs Sanjaykumar Ratilal Jaiswal Gujarat HC I (2001) DMC 19, (2000) 3 GLR 297** : 1. Husband's property are irrelevent for intermin maint. unless he is drawing income from them. 2. Wife is entitiled for free legal aid. She should not saddle lower middle calass husband with her Litigation expenses.

176. **Sanjay Bhardwaj & Ors. vs The State & Anr. Delhi HC 171 (2010) Delhi Law Times 644** : Unemployed man can not be forced to pay maintenence, Maint under DV to be ordered as per CrPC 125.

177. **Sanjay Sudhakar Bhosale vs Khristina Sanjay Bhosale Bombay HC 2008 Cri.L.J. (NOC) 833 (BOM.)** : No maintenance to wife under CRPC

125 if she can not prove Cruelty.

178. **Sanjeev Gupta vs Shalini Gupta Supreme Court 23 February 2009** : Interim maintenance increase illegal as no income proof produced.

179. **Sanjeev Kumar vs State Of U.P. Allahabad HC 30 September 2011** : Procedure for Arrest in Matrimonial Disputes.

180. **Saritha Rao & Ors. vs Y.Raghunath Rao & Anr Delhi HC CPC 169 (2010) DLT 277** : Husband lodged suit claiming damages on account of false prosecution after aquittal in 498A. Period of limitation is one year in a suit claiming damages on account of false prosecution and the period is calculated from the date when the false prosecution came to an end.

181. **Savita Sachin Sathone vs Sachin Matotrao Sathone Bombay HC 08 August 2016** : 1.It is well settled that if the material pleading is not denied or traversed, it is deemed to have been admitted. 2.wife threatening the husband of pouring kerosene on herself and of falsely implicating by making complaints against him and his family members in the Police Station, tantamount to cruelty. 3. no husband would like to hear that he was impotent for about 6 to 7 months after the marriage, if that was not true. Such an allegation would surely hurt a man's ego.

182. **Savitri Devi vs Ramesh Chand And Ors Delhi HC 2003 CriLJ 2759, 104 (2003) DLT 824, II (2003) DMC 328, 2003 (69) DRJ 6** : Courts admits misuse of 498A in many cases and send some advisories to Govt.

183. **Sejal Dharmesh Ved VS State of Maharashtra Bombay HC 07 March 2013** : DV cant be filed after 1 year of Separation.

184. **Sejalben Tejasbhai Chovatiya vs State of Gujarat Gujarat HC 20 October 2016** : Wife declaring completely incorrect facts and also suppressing the material aspect was prosecuted for perjury.

185. **Shaik Riayazun Bee vs The State Of A.P. Andhra HC 01 June 2016** : Relative of the husband for the purpose of Section 498A means related by blood, marriage or adoption.

186. **Shailja vs Khobbanna Supreme Court 18 January 2017** : Judgement against Husband = Whether the wife is capable of earning or whether she is actually earning are two different requirements.

187. **Shakti Pershad vs Ratna Pershad Delhi HC 2003 IAD Delhi 697, 102 (2003) DLT 756, 2003 (66) DRJ 580, 2003 RLR 176 :** HMA moveable property can not be termed as Income.

188. **Shakuntala Kumari v. Om Prakash Ghai Delhi HC AIR 1983 Delhi 53, 19 (1981) DLT 64** : False complaint by the wife to the husband's employer would amount to mental cruelty.

189. **Shamsher Singh Verma vs State Of Haryana Supreme Court 2015 (12) Scale 597** : 1. CD is a 'document' within the meaning of Section 3 of the Indian Evidence Act 2. Accused can play the CD in court in his defense.
190. **Shanavas vs Raseena Kerala HC 10 December 2010** : Magistrate cannot order non bailable warrant for the failure to pay maintenance.
191. **Shantabai vs Tarachand Madhya Pradesh HC HMA 12 1(a) 22 April 1965 AIR 1966 MP 8** : Although the Wife is not structurally or psychologically incapable of allowing sexual intercourse generally, yet she has an uncontrollable aversion to allowing coitus to the petitioner-husband. This case belongs to the rare variety of frigidity quoad hanc.
192. **Sharad Kumar Pandey vs Mamta Pandey Delhi HC 01 September 2010** : jurisdiction of the court would not be there where an aggrieved person starts residing deliberately only for the purpose of filing a case under domestic violence against respondent while the place has no relevance.
193. **Shashi vs Sunny Bhumbla Punjab-Haryana HC 25 January 2010** : Wife was earning and she suppressed and gave wrong affidavit hence Perjury.
194. **Shaukin vs State Of U.P. And Others Allahabad HC 11 October 2011, :** 1. Compliance of sections 41(1)(b) and 41 A Cr.P.C and to refrain from routinely arresting persons wanted in cases punishable by imprisonment up to 7 years. 2. Under section 498A IPC where the wife has gone back to her "maika", it may not be necessary in a particular case to immediately arrest the husband and other family members until adequate evidence has been collected, as she is unlikely to encounter violence when she is away from her "sasural. 3. Strong reasons are needed for arresting an accused with respectable antecedents, who is an income tax payee with roots in the community, and a permanent abode, no history of earlier abscondance or non-cooperation with the police and who is not likely to tamper with the evidence or to again commit a crime unless he is immediately arrested 4. Contempt of court and Disciplinary proceedings against the police who do not adhere to sections 41(1)(b) and 41 A Cr.P.C.
195. **Shiv Kumar Yadav vs Santoshii Yadav Chattisgarh HC CrPC 125 04 February 2004** : Wife wants to reside separately without sufficient cause, hence Maint denied.
196. **Shobha Rani vs Madhukar Reddi Supreme Court 1988 AIR 121, 1988 SCR (1)1010** : Husbands parents demanded dowry which was crulety on wife thus wife got divorce on Cruelty.

197. **Sudha Devi & Another vs State Of U.P. & Another Allahabad HC 02 April 2014** : Maint order to be paid from the date of order unless explicitly mentioned to pay from date of application.
198. **Shriram Munjaji Raut vs The State Of Maharashtra Bombay HC14 March 2011** : Rigorous imprisonment on Perjury for false evidence.
199. **Subhash Chand vs State(Delhi Administration) Supreme Court (2013) 2 SCC 17** : a complainant can file an application for special leave to appeal against an order of acquittal of any kind only to the High Court. He cannot file such appeal in the Sessions Court.
200. **Subhash Chandra Das Chowdhury vs Sandhya Das Chowdhury Calcutta HC 18 July 2008 (2008) 3 WBLR (Cal) 815**. : Once a matrimonial suit has been filed, the wife has no right to have a force entry in the house of her husband against his will if she is provided with maintenance by the husband.
201. **Sudha Suhas Nandanvankar vs Suhas Ramrao Nandanvankar Bombay HC AIR 2005 Bom 62, 2005 (1) BomCR 591, 2004 (4) MhLj 1052** : No Stridhan and Alimony and Annulment on Hiding Past. Marriage expenses cant be returned.
202. **Sujit Kumar vs Vandana Delhi HC 08 September 2016** : Eleven points to consider for int maint.
203. **Sukhdev Kaur vs Ravinder Singh Grewal Calcutta HC 18 July 1996 II (1997) DMC 69** : Divorce on Cruelty.
204. **Suman Kapur vs Sudhir Kapur Supreme Court 07 November 2008 (2009) 1 SCC 422** : The letters and entries in diary of wife, it was proved that there was mental cruelty on the part of the wife.
205. **Suman Singh vs Sanjay Singh Delhi HC 23 May 2013 2013 (5) RCR (Civil) 844** : Wife's allegations of dowry harassment, 498A/ 406, DV Act proven false, her evidence doesn't prove allegations; cruelty and divorce to husband.
206. **Sumana Bhasin VS Neeraj Bhasin Delhi District Court 27 May 2015** : wrongdoers should not get benefit out of frivolous litigations. all interim orders stand cancelled and wife was fined for false litigation.
207. **Sundar Babu & Ors vs State Of Tamil Nadu Supreme Court (2009) 14 SCC 244** : SC Explains Conditions For The Quash Of An FIR.
208. Sunder Singh vs Manna Sunder Singh Punjab-Haryana HC AIR 1962 Punj 127 : Wife alleged high income and property of husband but not proof was given by wife or husband.

209. **Sunil Kumar Gupta Vs. Shalini Gupta Uttarakhand HC 2012(4) Crimes 199 (Uttar)** : Right to Residence after Divorce to be decided based on Divorce Terms.
210. **Sunitha vs State Of Kerala Kerala HC 2011 [1] KLT 210** : Respondent in DV cant be arrested unles committed breach of a protection order.
211. **Sunny Paul & Anr. vs State Nct Of Delhi & Ors Delhi HC** : Senior Citizen Act Abusive son to be evicted from parents' home.
212. **Suo Motu Vs. Ushaben Kishorbhai Mistry Gujarat HC DMC20161587 , LAWS(GJH)2015 1171** : Detailed Discussion on Civil and Criminal Jurisdiction of DV. Application for DV quashing allowed by CrPC 482.
213. **Surbhi Agrawal vs Sanjay Agrawal Madhya Pradesh HC AIR 2000 MP 139, I (2000) DMC 453** : Divorce on Cruelty.
214. **Sushila Devi vs Shri Joginder Kumar Delhi HC 02 July 2010** : Maint to be decided on Actual Earning of husband and not on his parent's properties.
215. **Swati Kaushik vs Ashwini Sharma Delhi District Court 12 March 2015** : Equally qualified spouse, Maint for one year only then wife to find job.
216. **Sweety Gupta Vs Neety Gupta & Ors Delhi HC 25 October 2016** : 1.Serving Summon 2.On Whom Burden Of Proof Lies 3.Court May Presume Existence Of Certain Facts.
217. **Syed Nazim Husain vs Additional Principal Judge Family CourtAllahabad HC -Lucknow 09.01.2003:** Perjury application must be decided first before proceeding with the case.
218. **T K Surendran Vs P.Najima Bindu Kerala HC DMC2012249** : Judgement Against Husband = CrPC 125 and HMA 25 is applicable for Voidable Marriage.
219. **Umesh Kumar vs State Of A.P.And Anr Supreme Court (2013) 10 SCC 591** : Illegally obtained evidence is admissible.
220. **Urmila Devi vs Narinder Singh Himachal Pradesh HC AIR 2007 HP 19, 2006 (2) ShimLC 445** : 1. Wife is psychologically impotent and the marriage has not been consummated due to this reason, 2. Concealment of material fact.
221. **V. Bhagat vs D. Bhagat Supreme Court 1994 AIR 710, 1994 SCC (1) 337** : Irretrievable breakdown of the marriage.
222. **V.B.Kamalanathan vs K.Jayasree Madras HC 29 April 2016** : Upon non-payment of arrears, arrest cannot be ordered simply just because wife has asked for, the Court has to be satisfied that Husband despite having sufficient means had wilfully evaded the payment of arrears of

maintenance.

223. **Vanamala vs Shri H.M.Ranganatha Bhatta Supreme Court 1995 SCC (5) 299, JT 1995 (5) 670** : Mutual Divorced wife eligible for Maint.
224. **Vandana J. Kasliwal vs Jitendra N. Kasliwal Bombay HC AIR 2007 Bom 115, II (2007) DMC 227** : Wife was suffering from schizophrenia. This material fact concealed hence Annulment. Wife may seek Alimony.
225. **Varinder Kaur vs Jitender Kumar And Anr Punjab-Haryana HC 21 October 2016** : Daughter in law has no right to live in the self-acquired property of Parent in-laws.
226. **Varun Malik vs Payal Malik Delhi HC 2011(1) Crimes (Del) 496** : Family members of husband cannot be accused in DV case when they did not share household.
227. **Vidhya Viswanathan vs. Kartik Balakrishnan AIR 2015 SC 285** : not allowing a spouse for long time to have sexual intercourse by his or her partner, without sufficient reason, itself amounted to mental cruelty, hece divorce, But with huge Alimony.
228. **Vijay Dhanuka Etc vs Najima Mamtaj Etc Supreme Court (2014) 14 SCC 638** : an obligation is cast on the learned Magistrate to ensure before summoning the accused who resides beyond his jurisdiction, to make necessary enquiry.
229. **Vijay Kumar Vs. Harsh Lata Delhi HC 10 September 2008** : Equally qualified and equally earning wife, no interim maint.
230. **Vijay Verma v. State N.C.T. of Delhi & anr.Delhi HC 2010(3) LRC 291(DEL)** : Only violence committed by a person while living in the shared household can constitute domestic violence.
231. **Vijaya Baskar vs Suganya Devi Madras High Court MANU/TN/3477/2010** : Magistrate should not blindly call all family members as accused.
232. **Vikas Jain vs Deepali Jain Uttarakhand HC 25 October 2010** : No Maintenance u/s125Crpc for working Women.
233. **Vikas Kumar vs State of Bihar Supreme Court 18 July 2016** : Condition of paying maintenance to wife for AB is not sustainable in law.
234. **Vinita Devangan v. Rakesh Kumar Devangan Chattisgarh HC 2010(1) HLR 604** : 2010(1) AICLR 508 : 2009(3) Crimes 57 :2009(2) DMC 833 : Wife took MCD then filed 125, but Wife is a proprietor of a Boutique and she hide this fact, hence maintainence denied due to unclean hands.
235. **Vinita Saxena vs. Pankaj Pandit Supreme Court (2006) 3 SCC 778 :** regarding legal proposition on aspect of cruelty.

236. **Vinny Parmar vs Paramvir Parmar Supreme Court AIR 2011 SCC 2748** : For permanent alimony and maintenance income and property of both, are relevant material in addition to the conduct of the parties and other circumstances of the case.
237. **Vishwanat vs Sarla Vishwanath Agrawal Supreme Court AIR 2012 S.C. 2586** : Divorce on Cruelty but with Huge Alimony.
238. **Yamunabai Anantrao Adhav A vs Ranantrao Shivram Adhav Supreme Court 1988 AIR 644, 1988 SCR (2) 809** : Personal Law to be considered while deciding CrPC 125.

CHAPTER II

C.R.P.C Important Case Laws

CRIMINAL PROCUDURE CODE IMPORTANT CASE LAWS LIST

1. **Attiq-Ur-Rehman Vs.Municipal Corporation of Delhi and anotherAIR1996SC1267** : Cr.P.C. S.4 In absence of special court the regular court can try the offence
2. **Thomas Dana Vs.The State of PunjabAIR1959SC375** : Cr.P.C. S.4 The words Punishment and Penalty are explained in
3. **Republic of Italy thr. Ambassador and Ors.Vs.Union of India (UOI) and Ors.2013(1)SCALE462** : Cr.P.C. S.4 Union Govt was directed to constitute special court
4. **Pankajbhai Nagjibhai Patel vs. The State of Gujarat and Anr.AIR2001SC567** : Cr.P.C. S.4(2) When the special statute does not prescribe procedure Cr.P.C. is applicable.
5. **Sikandarkhan Mahomedkhan 1920(22)BOMLR200** : Cr.P.C. S.9 Additional Sessions Judge can hear appeal.
6. **The State of Bihar vs Chandra Bhushan Singh & Ors. AIR 2001 Supreme Court 429:** Cr.P.C. S.2(d) Charge sheet by RPF officer for offence under Railway Property Act can be treated as complaint of the RPF.
7. **Emperor Vs.Lakshman Chavji NarangikarAIR1931Bom313** : Cr.P.C. S.9(3) 194 and 409 Assistant and Additional Sessions Judges exercise jurisdiction of Sessions Court but they are separate Courts.
8. **Praphakar Vs. The State of Maha 2012 Cri.L.J.4726** : Cr.P.C. S.28 Assistant Sessions Judge should not be allotted with case punishable with more than 10 years.
9. **Pankajbhai Nagjibhai Patel vs The State Of Gujarat AIR 2001 SC 567** : Cr.P.C. S.29 and S.138 NI Act Magistrate has no pecuniary limit for compensation.
10. **Pankajbhai Nagjibhai Patel vs The State Of Gujarat AIR 2001 SC 567**: Cr.P.C. S.29 Magistrate has no pecuniary limit for compensation.
11. **Shidlingappa Gurulingappa Vs. EmperorAIR1926Bom416** : Cr.P.C. S.31 Aggregate fine should be considered for the purpose of appeal.

12. **Chatar Singh vs State Of M.P.AIR2007SC319 :** Cr.P.C. S.31 Aggregate sentence not to exceed 14 years when consecutive SC says.
13. **Hariom @ Kalicharan Shiriram and anr Vs. the State of Maharashtra 1994(2) Bom C.R.219:** Cr.P.C. S.31 and 427(1) Accused convicted in 3 cases His sentence of 22 years brought down by giving concurrence in two cases.
14. **Emperor vs Piru Rama Havaldar27 BOMLR 1371:** Cr.P.C. S.31 and IPC S.71 separate sentences are subject to the provisions of Section 71, Indian Penal Code.
15. **Jagat Bahadur Singh Jagat Bahadur Singh Vs .State of Madhya Pradesh, AIR 1966 SC 945** : Cr.P.C. S.31 Appellate court can inflict the Trial Court's limited punishment only
16. **Reg. Vs.Tukaya Bin TamanaILR1875 1 Bom 214 :** Cr.P.C. S.31 For S.457 and 380 IPC Sentence may be either for both or for one but should not greater.
17. **Sunil Anandrao Sawant vs Government Of Maharashtra 2010CriLJ3579:** Cr.P.C. S.31 Separate sentence to run consecutive after life has been discussed.
18. **Nanak Chand Vs.The State of PunjabAIR1955SC274 :** Cr.P.C. S.34 AND 149 Distinction is explained.
19. **Detention D.K. Basu Vs State of West Bengal AIR 1997 SC 610 :** Cr.P.C. S.41 and Constitution A.21 Directions w.r.t. arrest and
20. **R.P. Vaghela Vs. State of Gujarat2002CriLJ3082** : Cr.P.C. S.41 and Contempt of Courts Act S.10 Mere handcuffing without prior permission, in justifiable circumstances does not amount to contempt.
21. **Afak Shabbir Khan vs The State Of Maharashtra & Anr 2013BomCR(Cri)242(DB)** : Cr.P.C. S.41 Mentioning reasons in the arrest panchanama is held sufficient compliance of recording reasons for arrest.
22. **Arnesh Kumar Vs.State of BiharAIR2014SC2756 :** Cr.P.C. S.41(1) and 41A and S.498A of IPC Directions to police and Magistrates.
23. **Manikandan Vs. S. I. of Police, Nallalam Police Stn 2008CriLJ1338** : Cr.P.C. S.41(1)(d) Accused needs to bailed or not is discussed.
24. **Joginder KumarVs.State of U.P. and Ors.(1994)4SCC260** : Cr.P.C. S.56(1) Magistrate to ensure compliance of directions given.
25. **Jayendragiri Anandgiri Goswami Vs. Narcotics Control Bureau and Anr.2005CriLJ3190:** Cr.P.C. S.57 Accused in NCB custody arrested in another crime should be produced before magistrate within 24 hours.

26. **Gajanan P. Lasure Vs. The Director General of Police and ors 2009(4) Mh.L.J.399 :** Cr.P.C. S.57 and deemed suspension of accused public servant.
27. **Raghuvansh Dewanchand Bhasin Vs. State of Maharashtra and AnrAIR2011SC339 :** Cr.P.C. S.70 and 71 No Arrest on cancelled warrant. Warrant register be maintained.
28. **State Through Cbi vs Dawood Ibrahim Kaskar AIR1997SC2494 :** Cr.P.C. S.73 Warrant can be issued before charge sheet and for investigation purpose.
29. **Shaikh Raheman Vs. State of Maharashtra1991(1)Bom CR263 :** Cr.P.C. S.79 Magistrate can issue warrant for execution beyond his local jurisdiction.
30. **M.P. Sharma and Ors.Vs.Satish Chandra AIR1954SC300 :** Cr.P.C. S.93 and 94 Search and Seizure from accused not violative of fundamental rights.
31. **State of Gujarat Vs. Shyamlal Mohanlal Choksi MANU-SC-0383-1964 :** Cr.P.C. S.94 is not applicable to accused.
32. **State of Gujarat Vs. Shyamlal Mohanlal Choksi AIR 1965 SC 1251:** Cr.P.C. S.94(1) Power to issue summons to produce document is not applicable to accused.
33. **Pravinsingh and another Vs. Biharilal Singh and another 1989 Cri LJ 1386) (Bom):** Cr.P.C. S.97 Search can be conducted in a place other than mentioned in warrant.
34. **State Govt. of NCT of Delhi Vs. Sunil and Another, 2001 Cri.L.J. 504:** Cr.P.C. S.100 and S.27 Evi Act Witnesses not required.
35. **Khet Singh Vs Union of India (UOI)AIR2002SC1450:** Cr.P.C. S.100 Seizure panchanama prepared at customs office instead of spot did not cause prejudice Hence relied.
36. **State Of Maharashtra & Ors.Vs.Sudhir Vasant Karnataki Etc. Etc.MANU-SCOR 47069-2014:** Cr.P.C. S.100 Whether immovable property is included or not referred to larger bench.
37. **State Govt. of NCT of DelhiVs.Sunil and Another2001CriLJ504 :** Cr.P.C. S.100(5) and Evi Act S.27 Witnesses is not required.
38. **Bombay HC Full bench Sudhir Vasant Karnataki Vs. The State of Maharashtra 2011 (1) Bom.C.R. (Cri.) 326 _ 2011 ALL MR (Cri) 96 :** Cr.P.C. S.102(1) Property does not include immovable property.
39. **Sunder Singh vs State Of Uttar Pradesh AIR1956SC411 :** Cr.P.C. S.103 Applicable to search of a place and not of a person. Hence, independent

witnesses not necessary

40. **Suresh Nanda Vs. C.B.I.AIR2008SC1414 :** Cr.P.C. S.104 Passport can be impounded by Passport Authority and not by Police.
41. **The State of Maharashtra and Anr. Vs. Mangali Dewaiyya Pupalla1994MhLJ483** : Cr.P.C. S.107 and 116 No provision to ask for interim bond.
42. **Rajesh Suryabhan Nayak Vs. The State of Maharashtra 2006(5)MhLj243** : Cr.P.C. S.107 and 123 No interim bond and CJM reduced bond.
43. **Pramila Navin Shah Vs. State of Maharashtra & Ors2005(15)CriminalCC1051:** Cr.P.C. S.107 No provision to ask for interim bond.
44. **Dattatraya Mahadu Tikkal Vs. The State of Maharashtra2014(1)BomCR(Cri)439:** Cr.P.C. S.107 Sessions Judge has to interfere if action is illegal.
45. **Pravin Vijaykumar Taware,Vs.The Special Executive Magistrate 2009(111)BOMLR3166** : Cr.P.C. S.116 Training to Executive Magistrates directed by High Court
46. **Rajesh Suryabhan Nayak Vs.The State of Maharashtra, 2006(5)MhLj243 :** Cr.P.C. S.123(2) and (3) CJM exercised jurisdiction.
47. **Noor Saba Khatoon Vs. Mohd. Quasim AIR 1997 SC 3280** : Cr.P.C. S.125 and S.3 of MWPOD Act Rights of mior children and unmarried daughter are protected.
48. **Mohd. Ahmed Khan Vs. Shah Bano Begum and OrsAIR1985SC945** : Cr.P.C. S.125 applicable to Muslim divorced women also.
49. **Allabuksh Karim Shaikh Vs. Smt. Noorjahan Allabuksh Shaikh and another1994MhLJ1376** : Cr.P.C. S.125 application for muslim child is tenable
50. **Smt. Saroj Govind Mukkawar Vs. Smt. Chandrakalabai Polshetwar 2009(4)MhLj665** : Cr.P.C. S.125 Daughter in law was directed to maintain mother in law.
51. **Nandlal Wasudeo BadwaikVs.Lata Nandlal Badwaik and Anr.AIR2014SC932** : Cr.P.C. S.125 DNA Test prevails over the presumption.
52. **Bakulabai and Anr.Vs.Gangaram and Anr.(1988)1SCC537** : Cr.P.C. S.125 Illegitimate child is entitled for maintenance.
53. **Jaiminiben Hirenbhai Vyas Vs. Hirenbhai Rameshchandra VyasDecided On_ 19.11.2014** : Cr.P.C. S.125 Judgment shall contain

reasons for finding for grant of maintenance from the date of application.

54. **Jagdish Jugtawat Vs.Manju Lata and Ors.(2002)5SCC422** : Cr.P.C. S.125 Maintenance by Family Court to major daughter was upheld.
55. **Shivaji Baburao Bhabad @ Bhawad Vs. Sau. Alka Shivaji Bhabad Criminal Writ Petition No. 955 of 2009 decided on 14.01.2010:** Cr.P.C. S.125 Major son is not entitled for maintenance.
56. **Jagir Singh Vs. Ranbir Singh and Anr.AIR1979SC381:** Cr.P.C. S.125 Major son though student is not entitled for maintenance from father.
57. **Chinnappaiyan Chellandi Vs. Chinnathayee Chinnappaiyan2010(1) Crimes835** : Cr.P.C. S.125 Permission granted to amend petition.
58. **Sau. Manda R. Thaore Vs. Sh. Ramaji Ghanshyam Thaore Criminal Revision Application No. 317-2006Decided On_ 20.04.2010**: Cr.P.C. S.125 Second wifes maintenance rejected but compensation granted in revision.
59. **Syed Mohsin Ali Syed Shaukat Ali Vs. Smt. Noorus Saher MANU-MH-0996-2005**: Cr.P.C. S.125 Talaq must be for reasonable cause and be preceded by attempts at reconciliation.
60. **Savitaben Somabhai Bhatiya Vs. State of Gujarat and Ors.AIR2005SC1809**: Cr.P.C. S.125 Woman married by Hindu man having living spouse is not entitled for mainteance.
61. **Shantha @ Ushadevi and Anr.Vs.B.G. ShivananjappaAIR2005SC2410:** Cr.P.C. S.125(3) Successive applications are unnecessary and Limitation is not barred when the arrears upto date are included by interim application.
62. **Rajesh Bhiwaji Nande Vs. State of Maharashtra and Ors.2005(2)MhLj977 :** Cr.P.C. S.125(3) Successive orders of one month imprisonment upheld.
63. **Dalip Singh Vs.RajbalaII(2007)DMC273: Cr.P.C. S.125(4)** : Adultery defence not applicable after divorce.
64. **Dalip Singh Vs. RajbalaII(2007)DMC273 : Cr.P.C. S.125(4)** : Adultery not applicable to divorcee.
65. **Gita Vs. Chandrasekhar Cr.P.C. S.125(4)** : Divorced on cruelty ground is till entitled for maintenance.
66. **M. Chinna Karuppasamy Vs. Kanimozhi2015ALLMR(Cri)615 : Cr.P.C. S.125(4):** includes adultery by divorced wife.
67. **Chanda Preetam Wadate Vs. Preetam Ganpatrao Wadate 2002(2)MhLj482: Cr.P.C. S.125(4)** : Isolated instance of adultery is not sufficient to deny maintenance.

68. **Vanamala (Smt) Vs. H.M. Ranganatha Bhatta(1995)5SCC299 :** Cr.P.C. S.125(4) Wife does not include divorcee.
69. **Ashok Yeshwant Samant Vs. Smt. Suparna Ashok Samant and another1991CriLJ766:** Cr.P.C. S.127(1) Precondition to deposit arrears cannot be put.
70. **Ahmed Noormohmed Bhatti Vs. State of Gujarat and Ors.AIR2005SC2115:** Cr.P.C. S.151 is not ultravires merely because it can be misused.
71. **Ushaben Vs. Kishorbhai Chunilal Talpada and Ors.2012ACR1859:** Cr.P.C. S.154 and 198A Police can investigate S.494 with 498A of IPC as S.498A is cognizable.
72. **Anju Chaudhary Vs. State of U.P. and Anr.2013CriLJ776 :** Cr.P.C. S.154 and 156(3) If the offence is same there cannot be two FIRs. Magistrate can treat application as a complaint.
73. **Satvinder Kaur Vs.State (Govt. of N.C.T. of Delhi)AIR1999SC3596 :** Cr.P.C. S.154 and 177 The IO can forward the FIR to the police station having jurisdiction if the offence was beyond own jurisdictiono.
74. **Ganesha Vs. Sharanappa and anr.AIR2014SC1198 :** Cr.P.C. S.154 and 354 The person who lodges the FIR be called the Informant and not the Complainant.
75. **M. Narayandas vs State Of Karnataka And Ors.,2004 Cri.L.J. 822,:** Cr.P.C. S.154 FIR reasonableness or Credibility of the said information is not a condition precedent for registration of a case.
76. **Babubhai Vs. State of Gujarat and Ors.(2010)12SCC25 :** Cr.P.C. S.154 For deciding tenability of two FIRs sameness test should be applied.
77. **Ashi Devi and Ors.Vs. State (NCT of Delhi)MANU-SC-0526-2014 :** Cr.P.C. S.154 In a 9 years old theft case held that mere delay itself is not a ground to discard a case.
78. **Gosu Jayarami Reddy Vs. State of A.P. (2011) 11 SCC 766 :** Cr.P.C. S.154 Overwriting limited to converting 4 to 5 in FIR is immaterial.
79. **Ganesha Vs. Sharanappa and anr.2014(11)SCALE541 :** Cr.P.C. S.154 Person who lodges FIR is called Informant and who files complaint is called complainant.
80. **Mrs. Charu Kishor Mehta and etc.Vs.State of Maharashtra and Anr.2011CriLJ1486 :** Cr.P.C. S.154 Police cannot refuse to register the F.I.R. under the pretext of preliminary inquiry when cognizable offences are made out.

81. **Kumari Vs. Govt. of U.P. and Ors.2014CriLJ470** : Cr.P.C. S.154 Police is bound to register F.I.R. Lalita.
82. **Satish Narayan Sawant Vs. State of Goa2009CriLJ4655** : Cr.P.C. S.154 police officer going to the place of occurrence to make some survey does not amount to making an investigation doc.
83. **Mrs. Charu Kishor Mehta Vs. State of Maharashtra and Addl. Commissioner of PoliceDecided On_ 00.11.2010 :** Cr.P.C. S.154 Police shall register FIR instead of ignoring as civil dispute.
84. **Sone Lal And Ors AIR 1978 SC 1142** : Cr.P.C. S.154 Recording FIR is an official act and has such presumption.
85. **Charu Kishor Mehta and etc. etc.Vs.State of Maharashtra and Anr.2011CriLJ1486** : Cr.P.C. S.154 Reliability genuineness and credibility of the information are not the conditions precedent Mrs.
86. **M. Narayandas vs State Of Karnataka And Ors.,2004 Cri.L.J. 822** : Cr.P.C. S.154 Sections 195 and 340 do not come in the way of investigation by police. On the basis of such investigation the Court can file a complaint.
87. **Surender Kaushik and Ors. Vs. State of Uttar Pradesh and Ors.AIR2013SC3614 :** Cr.P.C. S.154 There cannot be two FIRs of the same person of same incident.
88. **Surender Kaushik and Ors.Vs.State of Uttar Pradesh and Ors.AIR2013SC3614 :** Cr.P.C. S.154 When a FIR is already there sameness test shall be used for the subsequent FIRs.
89. **State Of Haryana And Ors vs Ch. Bhajan Lal And Ors1992 AIR 604** : Cr.P.C. S.154 When can the Court pass appropriate orders.
90. **Satish Narayan Sawant Vs. State of Goa2009CriLJ4655** : Cr.P.C. S.154 When information was cryptic the police officer going to the place of occurrence to make some survey is not an investigation.
91. **Pravin Chandra Mody Vs. State of Andhra PradeshAIR1965SC1185** : Cr.P.C. S.155 Police can investigate a non cognizable offence under EC Act along with S.420 IPC.
92. **Dashrath Kishan Kotkar and Anr. Vs. State of Maharashtra1986MhLJ986** : Cr.P.C. S.155(2) and (3) Once permission is obtained the procedure applicable to cognazable offences is applicable.
93. **Vithal Puna Koli (Shirsath) and Ors. Vs. The State of Maharashtra-MH-0633-2006** : Cr.P.C. S.155(2) Obtaining Magistrate's permission is necessary.

94. **State of Maharashtra vs. Dharmendra Ambar Mohite (10.09.1998 - BOMHC)** : Cr.P.C. S.155(2) permission was not obtained Hence prosecution for offence of S.145 Police Act was held untenable.
95. **Mukhedkar Vs. The State of Maharashtra,1983CriLJ1833 :** Cr.P.C. S.155(2) Prosecution for S.124 of Bom Police Act quashed for want of permission Avinash Madhukar.
96. **Shivaji Vithalrao Bhikane Vs. Chandrasen Jagdevrao Deshmuk 2008CriLJ376** : Cr.P.C. S.156 and 397 156(3) of Cr.PC merely mean that an alleged cognizable offence should be investigated.
97. **Atul Son of Shridhar Kaple Vs. State of Maharashtra, through Police Station Officer2011 113 BOMLR1549 :** Cr.P.C. S.156 S.173(3) and s.190(1)(c).
98. **Pravin Chandra Mody Vs. State of Andhra PradeshAIR1965SC1185 :** Cr.P.C. S.156(1) and 173 Police officer can investigate E.C. Act offence along with S.420.
99. **Sheshrao and Ors. Vs. The State of Maharashtra and Ors.24.07.2015** : Cr.P.C. S.156(1) Charge sheet quashed for want of jurisdiction.
100. **Vinay TyagiVs.Irshad Ali @ Deepak and Ors. 2013CriLJ754** : Cr.P.C. S.156(3) and 173(8) Kinds of order under S.156(3) are (i) Initial Investigation, (ii) Further Investigation, (iii) Fresh or de novo or re-investigation-Detail.
101. **Satvinder Kaur Vs. State (1999)8SCC728** : Cr.P.C. S.156(2) Police can investigate any cognizable offence and to submit charge sheet before competent court.
102. **Alpic Finance Ltd. vs P. Sadasivan and Anr.AIR2001SC1226 :** Cr.P.C. S.156(3) and IPC S.420 It must also be shown that there existed a fraudulent and dishonest intention at the time of commission of the offence.
103. **Gopal Das Sindhi and Ors.Vs.The State of Assam and Anr.1961CriLJ39(3JJs) :** Cr.P.C. S.156(3) and 190 Passing order of S.156(3) or Search Warrant is not taking Cognizance.
104. **(R.R. Chari etc followed)Gopal Das Sindhi and Ors. Vs. The State of Assam and Anr.1961CriLJ39 :** Cr.P.C. S.156(3) and 190 Taking Cognizance on complaint means verification etc.
105. **Nirmaljit Singh Hoon Vs. The State of West BengalAIR1972SC2639** : Cr.P.C. S.156(3) and 200 Cognizance means not mere applying mind but for the purpose of proceeding under S.200 and following privisions.

106. **SachinVs.The State of Maharashtra2014ALLMR(Cri)1833** : Cr.P.C. S.156(3) and 200 Magistrate has discretion to reject the prayer and direct for verification etc.
107. Ramdev Food Products Private Limited Vs. State of Gujarat2015(3) SCALE622 : Cr.P.C. S.156(3) and 202 No arrest in investigation of S.202.
108. **Raghu Raj Singh Rousha Vs. Shivam Sundaram Promoters ((2009)2SCC363 :** Cr.P.C. S.156(3) and 397 Accused shall be impleaded in a revision against order refusing S.156.
109. **Shivaji Vithalrao Bhikane Vs. Chandrasen Jagdevrao Deshmuk2008CriLJ3761 :** Cr.P.C. S.156(3) and 398 Interference in revision should be in exceptional cases.
110. **Vasanti DubeyVs.State of Madhya Pradesh2012CriLJ1309** : Cr.P.C. S.156(3) and S.7 P.C. Act.
111. **Syed Muzaffaruddin Khan Mohd. Vs. Mohd.Abdul Qadir Mohd. Abdul. 2012 Bom C R(Cri) 375** : Cr.P.C. S.156(3) and S.195 and S.341 Magistrate can order S.156(3) and after investigation he can file complaint.
112. **Shivaji Vithalrao Bhikane Vs. Chandrasen Jagdevrao Deshmukh2008CriLJ3761** : Cr.P.C. S.156(3) and S.397 Direction by sessions judge for sending signature to the expert set aside.
113. **U.P. HC in Chandrika Singh Vs. State of U.P2007CriLJ3169 :** Cr.P.C. S.156(3) application can be treated as complaint.
114. **Mrs Priyanka Srivastava & Anr. Vs. State of UP & Ors2015 (96) SCC 287** : Cr.P.C. S.156(3) Application should be supported by affidavit.
115. **Shivaji Vithalrao Bhikane Vs. Chandrasen Jagdevrao Deshmukh2008CriLJ3761** : Cr.P.C. S.156(3) Before the order. complainant cannot be asked to call experto to prove forgery.
116. **Mohd. Yousuf Vs. Smt. Afaq Jahan and Anr.AIR2006SC705** : Cr.P.C. S.156(3) Complainant should not be examined before order under this section.
117. **Srinivas Gundluri and Ors. Vs. SEPCO(2010)8SCC206** : Cr.P.C. S.156(3) Difference of s.156(3) and 202 Cr.P.C. Mere direction to file charge sheet not illegal.
118. **Upkar Singh Vs. Ved Prakash and Ors.AIR2004SC4320** : Cr.P.C. S.156(3) Direction to register counter FIR is valid.
119. **Madhubala Vs. Sureshkumar AIR1997SC3104** : Cr.P.C. S.156(3) Format of order

120. **Anju Chaudhary Vs. State of U.P. and Anr.2013CriLJ776** : Cr.P.C. S.156(3) Magistrate can treat an application as a complaint In more than one FIRs sameness test has to be applied.
121. **CBI Central Bureau Of Investigation vs State Of Gujarat MANU-GJ-0573-2001** : Cr.P.C. S.156(3) Magistrate cannot direct.
122. **Central Bureau of Investigation through S.P., Jaipurvs.State of Rajasthan & Anr.AIR2001SC668** : Cr.P.C. S.156(3) Magistrate cannot direct the CBI investigation.
123. **K. Selvaraj Vs. The Superintendent of Police and The Inspector of Police** : Cr.P.C. S.156(3) Magistrate cannot order investigation by the CBI.
124. **Sachin Raosaheb Jadhav Vs State of Maharashtra Justice Nalawade** : Cr.P.C. S.156(3) Magistrate has discretion not to refer to police and to inquire himself into the application.
125. **Sukhwasi son of Hulasi Vs. State of Uttar Pradesh 2008 Cri.L.J.472** : Cr.P.C. S.156(3) Magistrate has discretion to send or not to send for investigation.
126. **Nilesh Daulatrao Lakhani Vs. State of Maharashtra2014(4)BomCR(Cri)757** : Cr.P.C. S.156(3) No cognizance on police report after first directing for inquiry.
127. **R.P. Kapur vs. S.P. Singh AIR 1961 SC 1117** : Cr.P.C. S.156(3) No order to CBI by Magistrate.
128. **Basanthi Sarkar and Ors.Vs.State of West Bengal and Ors.MANU-WB-0218-2010** : Cr.P.C. S.156(3) order in S.193 IPC offence upheld by Kolkata HC.
129. **Blue Dart Express Ltd. Vs.The State of Maharashtra2011(2)Crimes46** : Cr.P.C. S.156(3) order after verification was set aside and directed to proceed.
130. **Yogiraj Vasantrao Surve Vs. State of Maharashtra2013ALLMR(Cri)2059** :Cr.P.C. S.156(3) order can be challenged in Revision.
131. **R.R. Chari Vs. The State of Uttar Pradesh, AIR 1951 SC 207** : Cr.P.C. S.156(3) Order does not amount to taking cognizance 3 Judges Bench.
132. **General Officer Commanding Vs. CBI and Anr.AIR2012SC1890** : Cr.P.C. S.156(3) order is not taking cognizance.
133. **Shivaji Vithalrao Bhikane Vs. Chandrasen2008CriLJ3761** : Cr.P.C. S.156(3) Orders interference by superior Courts normally be in very exceptional circumstances.

134. **Ajit Ramrao Thete and others Vs. the State of Maharashtra and another Bombay (DB)** : Cr.P.C. S.156(3) Original Complaint and order should be retained in Court.
135. **Mohd. Yousuf Vs. Smt. Afaq Jahan and Anr.2006(1)KLJ380** : Cr.P.C. S.156(3) Petition's Format and nomenclature is not material It can be treated as complaint.
136. **Samaj Parivartan Samudaya and Ors. Vs. State of Karnataka and Ors.AIR2012SC2326** : Cr.P.C. S.156(3) Police investigation may start with registration of FIR while in other cases (CBI, etc.), an inquiry may lead to registration of an FIR.
137. **Laxminarayan Vishwanath Arya The State of Maharashtra through Senior Inspector of Police and Ors.Vs.2008CriLJ1** : Cr.P.C. S.156(3) Police need not seek permission of Magistrate to arrest accused.
138. **Raghu Raj Singh Rousha Vs. Shivam Sundaram Promoters (P) L and Anr.(2009)2SCC363** : Cr.P.C. S.156(3) Refusing direction for investigation and direction for verification and statements is taking cognizance.
139. **Karnataka HC Sri. B.V. Acharya, Vs. Sri. N. Venkateshaiah** : Cr.P.C. S.156(3) Sanction needed for even order under section.
140. **Mr. Panchabhai Popotbhai Butani, Vs. The State of Maharashtra 2010 Cri.L.J. 2723** : Cr.P.C. S.156(3) Simplicitor application without FIR is tenable.
141. **Pinni Co-op Housing Society and others Maruti Mathu Gaikwad and others Bom DB dd on 02.07.2013CRAPPLN463510** : Cr.P.C. S.156(3) This section cannot be resorted to after direction to put up for verification.
142. **Sakiri Vasu Vs. State of U.P. and Ors.AIR2008SC907** : Cr.P.C. S.156(3) When can Magistrate Monitor investigation.
143. **Maksud Saiyed Vs. State of Gujarat and Ors.(2008)5SCC66** : Cr.P.C. S.156(3) While passing the order the Magistrate has to apply mind.
144. **Rasiklal Dalpatram Thakkar Vs. State of Gujarat and Ors.AIR2010SC715** : Cr.P.C. S.156(5) and 181(4) Jurisdiction to be of the JMFC and not of the PSO.
145. **Mr. Panchabhai Popotbhai Butani Vs. The State of Maharashtra2010CriLJ2723** : Cr.P.C. S.156(6) Application without prior F.I.R. tenable. Cr.P.C. S.156(6) No inherent power to recall order.
146. **State rep. by Inspector of Police, Vigilance and Anti-Corruption, Tiruchirapalli, Tamil Nadu vs. V. Jayapaul (22.03.2004 -**

SC)(2004)5SCC223 : Cr.P.C. S.157 No statutory bar to the informant-police officer for taking up the investigation.

147. **The State of Uttar Pradesh Vs. Bhagwant Kishore JoshiAIR1964SC221** : Cr.P.C. S.157 and PC Act Investigation can be started on information or otherwise means without FIR.
148. **S.N. Sharma Vs. Bipen Kumar Tiwari and Ors.AIR1970SC786** : Cr.P.C. S.159 does not enable Magistrate to stop investigation.
149. **S.N. Sharma Vs. Bipen Kumar Tiwari and Ors.AIR1970SC786 :** Cr.P.C. S.159 Gives limited power to Magistrate to direct investigate proceed himself but no power to stop investigation.
150. **S.N. Sharma Vs. Bipen Kumar Tiwari and Ors.AIR1970SC786** : Cr.P.C. S.159 Meant to give Magistrate the power of directing investigation where the police decide not to investigate the case under the proviso to Section 157(1)
151. **Ashok Debbarma Vs. State of Tripura(2014)4SCC747** : Cr.P.C. S.161 and 154 Omission to name accused when he was part of group is not fatal.
152. **State of N.C.T. of Delhi Vs. Mukesh(2013)2SCC58** : Cr.P.C. S.161 and 162 and Evi Act S.145 Statement on TV channel subsequent to charge sheet is not covered Bipin Panchal distinguished.
153. **Mahesh Janardhan Gonnade Vs. State of Maharashtra(2008)13SCC271** : Cr.P.C. S.161 and 164 Testimony of I.O. and Spl Judl. Magi. cannot be disbelieved and discredited.
154. **Ashok Debbarma @ Achak DebbarmaVs.State of Tripura (2014)4SCC747 :** Cr.P.C. S.161 Every omission is not contradiction.
155. **Nirpal Singh and Ors.Vs. State of HaryanaAIR1977SC1066** : Cr.P.C. S.161 Statement of witness need not be there in inquest panchanama.
156. **State of Gujarat Vs. Kathi Ramku Aligbhai1986CriLJ239** : Cr.P.C. S.161 Inadmissible portions in the panchana should be marked by the APP and excluded by the Juge and How to appreciate witnesses.
157. **State of U.P. Vs. M.K.AnthonyAIR1985SC48.AnthonyAIR1985SC48** : Cr.P.C. S.161 Signature of witness does not render evidence inadmissible.
158. **Gujarat High Court Full Bench Nathu Manchhu Vs. The State of Gujarat1978CriLJ448** : Cr.P.C. S.161 Statement reading over to witness does not make his evidence inadmissible.
159. **Suresh Vs. The State of Maharashtra (DB) Decided On_ 31.10.2014** : Cr.P.C. S.161 Statement should not be read over to the witness by the

police.

160. **Md. Ankoos and Ors. Vs. The Public Prosecutor, High Court of A.P. AIR2010SC566** : Cr.P.C. S.161(3) Statement cannot be used.

161. **Dr. Sunil Clifford Daniel Vs. State of Punjab(2012)11SCC205** : Cr.P.C. S.161_ In view of exception of S.162(2) to S.161, statement of accused under S.27 Evi Act need not be signed by accused.

162. **State of Kerala Vs. Babu & OrsAIR1999SC2161** : Cr.P.C. S.162 and 161 and 91 Magistrate can call case diary of another case.

163. **Mr. Prakash Vernekar Vs. State of Goa2007CriLJ4649** : Cr.P.C. S.162 and 452 and S.27 not barred for deciding custody of muddemal.

164. Mr. Prakash Vernekar Vs. State of Goa 2007 Cri.L.J. 4649 : Cr.P.C. S.162 and S.27 Statement is not barred for deciding custody of muddemal.

165. **State of Karnataka by Nona vinakere Police Vs. Shivanna @ Tarkari Shivanna 2014(3)BomCR(Cri)98 (2014(3)BomCR(Cri)98)** : Cr.P.C. S.164 and IPC S.376 Directions to Police and Magistrates.

166. **Pakala Narayana Swami Vs. Emperor AIR1939PC47** : Cr.P.C. S.162 Any confession made to a police officer in course of investigation whether a discovery is made or not is excluded.

167. **Tahsildar Singh and Anr. Vs. The State of Uttar Pradesh AIR1959SC1012** : Cr.P.C. S.162 Contradictions an omissions.

168. **Ramkishan Mithanlal Sharma Vs. The State of Bombay AIR1955SC104** : Cr.P.C. S.162 covers statements to police during TIP.

169. **George & Ors vs State Of Kerala (1998) 4 SCC 605** : Cr.P.C. S.162 Statement of I.O. in the inquest what he saw is admissible.

Printed by Libri Plureos GmbH in Hamburg,
Germany